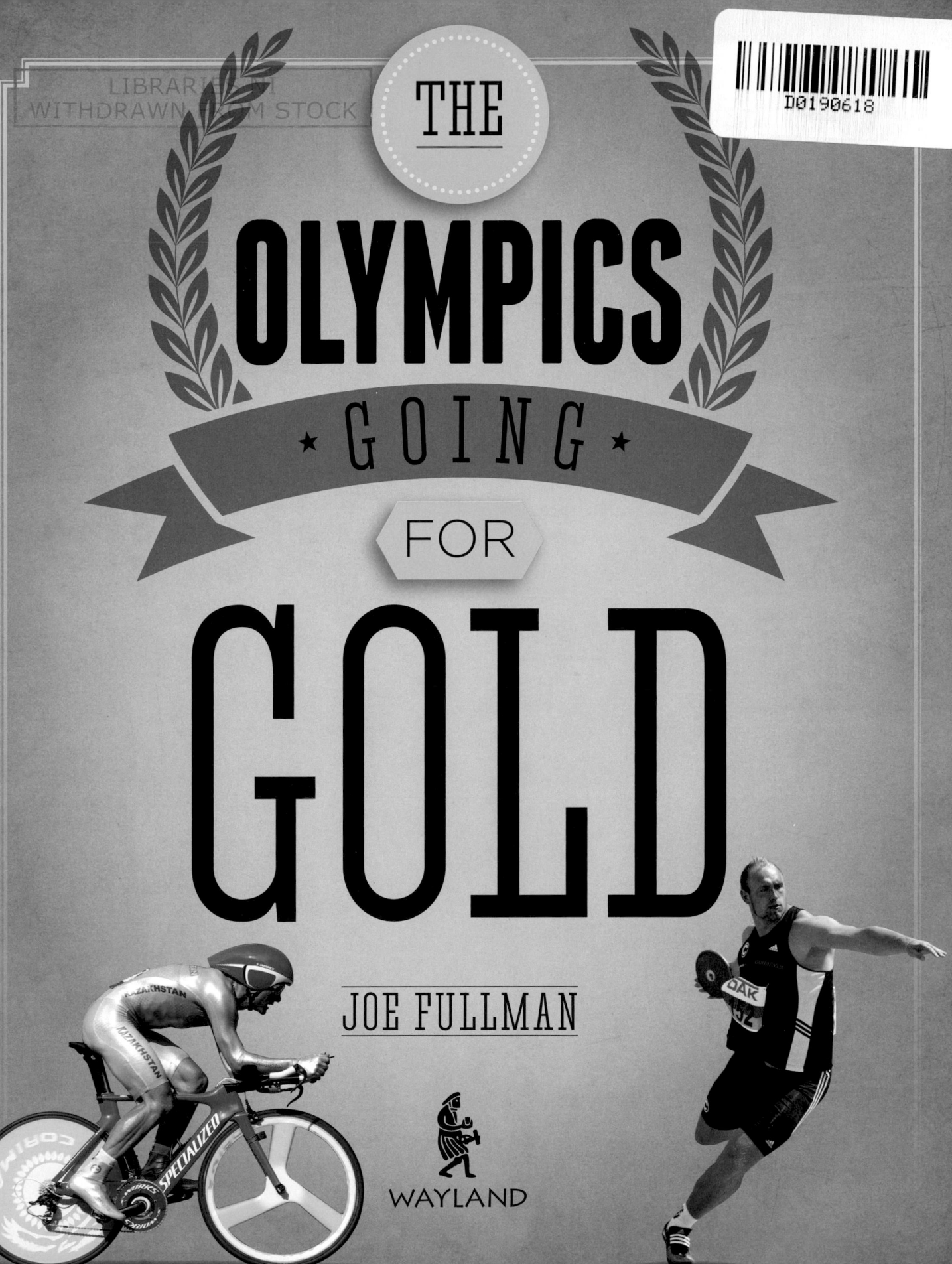

THE
OLYMPICS
★ GOING ★
FOR
GOLD

JOE FULLMAN

WAYLAND

LIBRARIES NI
WITHDRAWN FROM STOCK

D0190618

CONTENTS

A CELEBRATION
OF SPORT

The Summer Olympics are the biggest, most thrilling and most international sporting event in the world. Every four years, more than 10,000 athletes from over 200 countries get together to compete in a huge range of sports.

A global TV audience of more than four billion people tunes in to see incredible sporting performances, records being broken, and spectacular opening and closing ceremonies. In the host city itself, hundreds of thousands of spectators watch more than 300 events across 28 sports, covering everything from archery, boxing and cycling to swimming, tennis, and volleyball.

Many athletes have become global superstars following success at the Olympic Games. Jamaica's Usain Bolt, shown here, broke the world 100m and 200m records at the 2008 Beijing Olympics. He defended his titles at London four years later.

THE CHOSEN CITY
Staging the Olympics is a great way for a city to get international attention but it can be hugely expensive. The facilities for the London 2012 games, such as this stadium, cost £9 billion to construct, while the 2008 Beijing Olympics cost a staggering £29 billion, making it the most expensive Summer Games yet.

PREPARING FOR THE GAMES

Most of a host city's Olympic money is spent on new sporting venues. For the 2016 Rio de Janeiro Games, the organisers used some existing facilities, such as the Maracanã football stadium (right), but they also had to build an Olympic Park with 15 new venues.

The Olympics began in 776 BCE in Ancient Greece, where they were held every four years for more than a thousand years until 394 CE.

The Games were revived in 1896 by the French scholar and sportsman, Baron Pierre de Coubertin, who believed they could be used to bring nations together and promote peace. Since the first modern Olympics in Athens, Greece, there have been 31 summer Olympics held in 23 different cities in 19 different countries.

OPENING AND CLOSING CEREMONIES

The Olympics are opened and closed with spectacular ceremonies, featuring dancing, music and theatrical performances designed to showcase the culture of the host city. These are also the times when the Olympic Flame (seen here in Seoul in 1988), which burns throughout the competition, is first lit and then later extinguished.

RUNNING

The running, or 'track', events are often the highlight of the Olympic programme. In particular, the 100m competitions, for both men and women, are usually the most watched events.

6

THE SPRINTS

In the sprints, athletes start in a crouched position and use a device called 'blocks' to help them explode forwards when the gun goes off. Middle and long-distance runners start in a standing position.

All running events, apart from the main part of the marathon, are staged at the Olympic stadium around a 400m oval track. Races are always run anticlockwise, although no one is entirely sure why. It could be because most athletes have stronger right legs than left ones, and so it feels more 'natural' to run this way. Athletes wear special spiked shoes to grip the track, which is made out of a spongy substance called polyurethane.

The middle distance races are the 800m and the 1500m, which are run over several laps of the track. Runners often make a late sprint to claim victory. But at London 2012, David Radisha (below) of Kenya broke the 800m world record having led right from the start.

LONG DISTANCES

The long distance track races are the 5,000m (12.5 laps of the track) and 10,000m (25 laps of the track). These events take a long time – around half an hour for the 10,000m. During the races, the runners can become strung out in a long line, and slower athletes may even be lapped by the leaders.

THE MARATHON

The longest running race starts and finishes in the Olympic Stadium, but most of the marathon takes place out on the streets of the host city. Its distance of 26 miles, 385 yards, was set at the 1908 London games so that Queen Alexandra could watch the finish in front of the royal box at the Olympic Stadium.

The three shortest and fastest events are the 100m, which is run on a straight part of the track, the 200m, which starts on a curve and finishes on a straight, and the 400m, which is one lap of the track. The eagerly anticipated 100m finals are over in a flash. At London 2012, Usain Bolt won the men's event in an Olympic record of just 9.63 seconds.

OLYMPIC RUNNING EVENTS

(MEN AND WOMEN)

100 metres • 200 metres • 400 metres • 800 metres • 1500 metres • 5000 metres 10,000 metres • Marathon • 110 metres hurdles (for men) • 100 metres hurdles (for women) • 400 metres hurdles • 3000 metre steeplechase • 4 x 100 metres relay • 4 x 400 metres relay

OBSTACLE RACES

The 7.5 lap 3000m steeple chase is the most gruelling of the four Olympic hurdle races. On every lap, runners must jump over four large barriers and a water jump. Falls are common, particularly near the end when athletes are tired.

FIELD EVENTS

While running races are taking place on the track, a number of throwing and jumping events are staged in the field at its centre – which is why they're also called 'field events'.

The main grassy area of the field is divided into separate areas for the four throwing events: shot put, discus, hammer and javelin. Discus and hammer throwers compete within a three-sided net cage to prevent their throws from hitting people in the crowd. There are also run-ups and landing areas for the long jump, triple jump, high jump and pole vault.

8

LONG JUMP

The long jump was one of the ancient Olympic events. Back then competitors took off from a standing start. Today's long jumpers take long run ups and take off at full speed. At the Mexico Games in 1968, the USA's Bob Beamon (above) leapt 8.90m, a world record that would last over 23 years – it's still the Olympic record today.

High jumpers used to either jump forward or scissor kick their legs over the bar. But at Mexico 1968, Dick Fosbury won the gold medal for the USA by jumping backwards over the bar. His revolutionary technique, nicknamed the 'Fosbory Flop', is now used by all Olympic high jumpers.

FIELD EVENTS
(MEN AND WOMEN)

High jump • Pole vault
• Long jump • Triple jump
• Shot put • Discus throw
• Hammer throw • Javelin throw

POLE VAULT

The pole vault has been contested at every Olympics, although the women's competition was only introduced in 2000. In the early days, athletes used stiff wooden poles. Later, flexible carbon fibre poles were introduced which can propel the best vaulters over 6m into the air.

Many of the modern field events originated at the ancient Olympics, including the long jump, discus and javelin. There are some differences, however. Ancient athletes threw the javelin towards a target, whereas their modern counterparts try to throw it as far as possible. But perhaps the greatest difference is that ancient athletes were all men – and competed entirely in the nude.

DISCUS

During the discus competitions, athletes compete to see who can throw a heavy disc weighing 2kg (men) or 1kg (women) the farthest. Throwers, such as the 2012 Olympic champion, Robert Harting of Germany (right), spin round on the spot to build up speed and momentum before releasing the disc.

SWIMMING
AND DIVING

As with track and field, swimming races have been held since the first modern Olympics in 1896, although they didn't form part of the ancient games.

Most of today's Olympic swimming races are staged in a 50m pool in a purpose-built aquatics centre. However, at the first few Olympic swimming competitions, all races were held outside in open water. The Athens 1896 swimming events took place in the Mediterranean Sea. Today, only the marathon 10km and the swimming leg of the triathlon take place in open water.

DIFFERENT STROKES

Olympic swimmers race using four main strokes: front crawl, backstroke, breaststroke and butterfly. Although any stroke can be used for the 'freestyle' events, all competitors use the front crawl because this is the quickest stroke. Butterfly, which was only invented in the 1930s, was first featured in the 1956 Melbourne games. The above image shows a men's butterfly race from London 2012.

SUPER SWIMMERS

At the 1972 Munich Olympics, the US swimmer Mark Spitz won seven gold medals, a record. Many people though his feat would never repeated. But at Beijing 2008, another US swimmer, Michael Phelps (left), managed to win eight gold medals.

SWIMMING EVENTS
(MEN AND WOMEN)

50 metres freestyle • 100 metres freestyle •
200 metres freestyle • 400 metres freestyle •
1500 metres freestyle (men only) • 100 metres
backstroke • 200 metres backstroke •
100 metres breaststroke • 200 metres breaststroke •
100 metres butterfly • 200 metres butterfly •
200 metres individual medley • 400 metres individual
medley • 4 x 100 metres freestyle relay •
4 x 200 metres freestyle relay •
4 x 100 metres medley relay • marathon 10km

Olympic swimmers used to begin all their races in the water – and still do for the backstroke. Blocks, from which swimmers dive into the water to get as fast a start as possible, were introduced for the 1936 Berlin games. These days, men and women compete (separately) in the same events apart from the 1500m freestyle, which has historically been swum only by men – though a women's event may be added in the future.

Olympic divers perform acrobatic dives, often involving numerous twists and somersaults, from two boards: one 3 metres high, the other 10 metres high. Pairs of divers also take part in synchronized diving.

SYNC OR SWIM
Known in earlier times as 'water ballet', synchronized swimming is one of just two Olympic sports, along with rhythmic gymnastics, in which only women compete. Swimmers perform choreographed dance routines to music. The pool is even fitted with underwater speakers to help the swimmers stay in time.

GYMNASTICS

The vaulting, somersaulting, backflipping feats of the gymnasts are a highlight of every Summer Olympics. These acrobatic events are designed to demonstrate agility, coordination, balance and strength.

Until Amsterdam 1928, only men were allowed to compete in the Olympic gymnastic competition. Today, both sexes take part, but not in exactly the same events. There are six events for men (rings, parallel bars, horizontal bar, pommel-horse, vault and floor exercise) and four for women (vault, balance beam, uneven bars, floor exercise). The men's events tend to focus on strength and control, while the women's emphasise agility, flexibility and rhythm.

TEAM VERSUS INDIVIDUAL

The Olympic gymnastic competition is made up of both team events and individual events. In the team events, six gymnasts from each participating country perform on every piece of equipment. The team with the highest score wins.

ANCIENT GREEK GYMNASTICS

It was the Ancient Greeks who gave the sport its name. The 'Gymnasium' was the place where athletes trained. It comes from the word 'gymnos' meaning naked, as the athletes competed in the nude.

AZƏRBAYCAN 250m
POÇTU 1996

Olqa Korbut.
Qızıl medala çatma.
Sərbəst hərəkətlər.
Münhen. 1972-ci il.

BACKFLIP TO FAME

Olga Korbut from the Soviet Union revolutionised gymnastics with her performances at the Munich games of 1972. She was the first gymnast to perform a backward flip on the balance beam, and she also executed a special backward somersault on the parallel bars known as the 'Korbut flip' that no one had attempted before.

Only women compete in rhythmic gymnastics, as it is seen as a test of agility rather than power (though some people think men should compete too). Gymnasts perform routines using one of five pieces of apparatus: ball, hoop, ribbon, clubs and ropes.

The Olympics has seen some exciting gymnastics competitions – perhaps none more so than in 1996. The USA and Russia were battling for gold in the women's team competition. Everything came down to the last vault, but the US gymnast Kerri Strug had injured her ankle in the previous round. Bravely, she performed the vault, winning the gold medal for the US before collapsing to the floor in pain.

NADIA COMANECI

Another star emerged at the 1976 Montreal Olympics – Nadia Comaneci from Romania. Aged just 14, she was the first gymnast to be awarded a perfect 10 following her performances on the uneven bars and the beam. Because nobody thought such a high score was possible, the Olympic scoreboard didn't go up to 10.00, so it was actually displayed as 1.00.

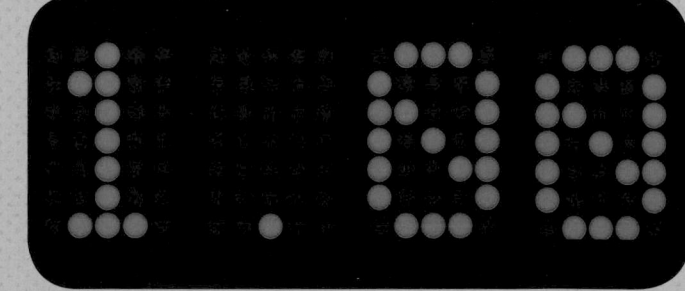

ROWING & SAILING

Sailors and rowers need to be strong and determined to battle the elements and come out on top at the Olympics. The sailing and rowing competitions are held in open water, often far away from the main Olympic Stadium.

Although scheduled for the 1896 Olympics, the sailing and rowing events were cancelled following fierce storms. They've featured at every Olympics since, though. Several types of boat compete in the Olympic sailing competitions, ranging from small dinghies to larger multi-hull boats. All events are 'fleet' format, whereby all the boats race at the same time on the same course. Sailing is one of the only Olympic sports where men and women compete directly against one another.

WINDSURFING

An Olympic sport since 1984, windsurfing was going to be replaced by kitesurfing at the 2016 games. However, the decision was reversed after protests from windsurfing federations. All windsurfers must use the same model of board at the Olympics to make the competition fair.

SAILING STARS

The Danish sailing master, Paul Elvstrom, competed in eight Olympics from 1928 to 1988 (the last when he was 60) winning four gold medals. His haul was eventually beaten by the British sailor Ben Ainslie (right) who won four golds and a silver at five Olympics between 1996 and 2012.

There are two types of Olympic rowing event, which are competed in by both men and women. In the single skulls, double skulls, and quadruple skulls, rowers use two oars, one on either side of the boat. In the coxless pairs, coxless fours, and eights, rowers use large 'sweep' oars, which they row on just one side of the boat. The largest boat, the eight, has a non-rowing member, the cox, who steers the boat.

CANOEING & KAYAKING

Although similar sports, there are slight differences between canoeing and kayaking. Canoeists paddle kneeling down, while kayakers sit and use a more curved paddle. Men and women compete in both at the Olympics, tackling races ranging from 200m to 1000m. There are two disciplines: sprints, which are raced on flatwater, and slalom events, such as the one shown here, where competitors paddle down a whitewater course between hanging gates.

MULTIPLE MEDALS

The five gold medals won by the British rower Sir Steve Redgrave between 1980 and 2000 represent one of the all-time great Olympic performances. But even this was overshadowed by the efforts of the German kayaker Birgit Fischer (right) who won eight gold medals between 1980 and 2004 – and she probably would have won more had East Germany, the country she then represented, not boycotted the 1984 Olympics.

CYCLING

There's a lot of two-wheel action at the Olympics with riders battling it out in 18 events in four different types of cycling: road cycling (4 events), track cycling (10 events), mountain biking (2 events) and BMX (2 events).

RACING HARD

At the BMX races, riders start in a straight line behind a manually operated gate. Falls and collisions are common in this rough, tough sport, so riders wear helmets, gloves and long-sleeved tops for protection.

Just a single road race and five track events were staged at the first modern Olympics in 1896, but gradually more events have been added to the programme. Women's road cycling was introduced in 1984, followed by women's track cycling in 1988. The first mountain bike competition was held in 1996, while the latest addition to the programme, BMX, made its debut at Beijing in 2008.

MUSCLE POWER

Track bikes don't have brakes or changeable gears, but are set permanently in the highest gear. They take a lot of muscle power to ride. Cycling has given the British athlete Sir Chris Hoy (left) enormous thighs with a circumference of 44cm. They powered him to six Olympic gold medals between 2000 and 2012.

ROAD RACERS

In the Road Race, all the riders start together and the first one to complete the course (250km for men, 140km for women) wins. The other road-racing discipline, the Time Trial, takes place over a 44 km (men) or a 29km (women) course, with riders starting 90 seconds apart. Whoever completes the course in the fastest time is the winner.

Road cycling takes place out on the streets of the host city. Track cycling is staged at a purpose-built centre called a velodrome where the tracks have steeply sloped sides to make the bikes travel faster. Mountain bikers have to contend with a rugged cross-country course, while BMX races take place on twisting circuits with lots of turns and bumps.

Time trial and track cycling are all about hitting the highest possible speeds. The bikes are extremely light and narrow to cut through the air, while the cyclists wear aerodynamic helmets and clothes, and tuck themselves into a streamlined position.

DIY

There is no official Olympic distance for the mountain biking events, but at London 2012 riders had to complete six laps of a 4.8km course. Unlike road racers, mountain bikers can receive no assistance during the race, so if they get a puncture they have to fix it themselves.

COMBAT SPORTS

For most athletes, bruises are an unfortunate part of their job. But for those that take part in combat sports, they're badges of honour – particularly if they belong to their opponents.

The five Olympic combat sports – boxing, wrestling, taekwondo, judo and fencing – have produced numerous multiple champions over the years. The Cuban boxer Félic Savón (1992–2000) won three gold medals as did the Greco Roman wrestler, Aleksandr Karelin (1988–2000).

TAEKWONDO

Taekwondo is a Korean martial art that translates as 'the art of foot and fist'. Two competitors battle using punches and kicks. The one who lands the most in three two-minute rounds, is declared the winner.

Fencers score points by hitting their opponent with the tip or the blade of their sword. The swords are wired up so that a buzzer sounds when a hit has been made. As the swords are sharp, fencers wear protective clothing, including a wire mesh face mask.

FREESTYLE V GRECO-ROMAN

Olympic wrestlers compete over three two-minute rounds during which they score points by throwing their opponent or pinning them down. There are two types of wrestling: freestyle, in which wrestlers can use all of their bodies; and Greco Roman (shown here) where they can use only those body parts above the waist.

STEPPING STONE TO GLORY

Unlike professional boxers, Olympic boxers wear protective headgear and box for just three rounds rather than the standard 12. Men box three-minute rounds, while women box two-minute rounds. Several Olympic boxers have gone on to have glittering professional careers, including Muhammad Ali, Sugar Ray Leonard and Floyd Mayweather Jr.

But the greatest multiple winner of all was the fencer Aladár Gerevich of Hungary. He won his first gold medal in 1932 aged 22, and his last 28 years later, aged 50. When he wasn't initially picked for the 1960 games, Gerevich challenged the entire Hungarian squad to duel. He beat everyone, forcing the Hungarian Olympic Committee to change its mind and let him take his place on the team.

JUDO

Judo bouts take place on a padded mat and last for 5 minutes. Competitors score points by throwing their opponent to the ground, pinning them on their back, or by putting them in a hold they can't get out of.

RACKETS
AND TARGETS

Incredible hand-eye coordination is required for the three Olympic racket sports – tennis, badminton and table tennis – while supreme marksmanship is the name of the game at the two target sports, archery and shooting.

The medal tables for these sports show how some nations have come to dominate certain events in recent times. Chinese athletes rule the table tennis and badminton competitions, winning every gold medal available at the 2012 games. Lin Dan, who won the males singles badminton gold in 2008 and 2012, is considered pretty special even by Chinese standards, and is perhaps the greatest badminton player of all time. South Korea has a hold on the archery events, claiming three out of four possible golds in 2012.

GOLDEN GEESE

Very special shuttlecocks are used in the Olympic badminton competitions. Each must weigh between 4.74g and 5.5g and have exactly 16 feathers picked from the left wing of a goose – so that they all lie in the same direction, which helps the shuttlecock to fly true.

At London 2012, the Swiss tennis player Roger Federer (right) played a marathon semi-final match, finally beating the Argentinean Juan Martin del Potro 19-17 in the final set. Federer lost to Britain's Andy Murray in the final.

HITTING THE TARGET

Olympic archers stand 70m away from a circular target which is divided into 10 rings, worth points from 1 (the white outer ring) to 10 (the yellow bullseye). Players go head to head in a knockout competition with every archer firing 12 arrows. They have 40 seconds to release each arrow.

CHOOSE YOUR WEAPON

There are 15 shooting events using three separate weapons (rifle, pistol and shotgun) fired at a variety of distances and targets. Rifle and pistol shooters fire at stationary 10-ring targets, while shotgun competitors try to hit clay targets flying through the air.

Female Korean archers are particularly renowned, having won six of seven individual Olympic titles between 1984-2012. But in tennis and shooting, the winners have been drawn from a much wider selection of countries.

CHINESE CHAMPIONS

Out of a possible 28 gold medals available since 1988, China has won a staggering 24. The table tennis competition used to feature singles and doubles matches. However, a team game, in which three players compete in four singles matches and a doubles match, replaced the doubles competition in 2008.

HORSES AND
HEAVYWEIGHTS

Non-human athletes get a chance to take part in the Olympics too in the Equestrian events, while the only human athletes possibly capable of lifting a horse strain their way to Olympic weightlifting glory.

EVENTING

Three-day eventing is probably the most taxing equestrian competition. On the first day, riders perform a dressage test, followed on the second day by a cross country ride over 45 jumps (points are knocked off for any mistakes made). The third day is a show jumping competition. The rider with the best score over all three days wins.

Along with sailing, equestrianism is the only Olympic sport in which men and women compete directly against one another. But then, the three equestrian events – dressage, eventing and show jumping – have always seemed a little different from the rest of the Olympic programme. It's a sport that often attracts wealthy, and sometimes even royal competitors. For instance, Princess Anne of the British royal family took part in 1976 and her daughter, Zara Phillips (left), won a silver medal at the team eventing competition in 2012.

Dressage, in which the horse and rider perform a sort of choreographed dance together in a sand arena, was originally a form of military training. Indeed, until 1952, only military officers were allowed to compete in the Olympic dressage competition.

POCKET HERCULES

Standing just 1.47m tall and weighing 62kg, the Turkish weightlifter Naim Suleymanoglu won Olympic gold in 1988, 1992 and 1996. At the 1988 games, he became the first man to lift three times his body weight above his head, making him, pound for pound, the strongest weightlifter in history.

The weightlifting events, to find the strongest humans on Earth, have been held at every modern Olympics (though the women's competition only began in 2000). These days all the events require the use of two hands, but in the early days of the Games, there was an event to see who could lift the heaviest weight one-handed.

WEIGHTLIFTING

In both the men's and the women's events, competitors perform two types of lift: the snatch, where the weight is lifted from the floor to above the head in a single motion; and the clean and jerk, where the weight is rested on the chest and then pushed above the head. The two heaviest weights successfully lifted are combined to give the final score.

SHOW JUMPING

The show jumping competition takes place on a course with around 15 fences. Riders compete against the clock, aiming to clear the fences in the fastest time. Time penalties are awarded if a horse knocks down a fence or if it refuses to make a jump.

TEAM SPORTS

The Olympics is also the stage for a number of team sports including water polo, volleyball (both beach and indoor), basketball, field hockey, football and handball.

The team sports have seen some of the most fiercely contested events in Olympic history. In 1956, shortly after the Soviet Union invaded Hungary, the two countries met in a bad-tempered Olympic water polo semi final. The teams fought throughout, and the match was eventually stopped when a Soviet player punched a Hungarian in the face, drawing blood. It became known as the 'Blood in the Water' game. The Hungarians won and went on to take gold, defeating Yugoslavia in the final.

FIELD HOCKEY

This fast-moving sport first featured at the Olympics in 1908 (1980 for women). India dominated during the early decades winning 8 out of 12 golds between 1928 and 1980. Dyhan Chand, often called 'the greatest hockey player of all time' once scored six goals in a single game when India played Germany in 1936.

STRONG SWIMMERS

Water polo players have to be very good swimmers with a lot of stamina, as they are not allowed to touch the bottom or the sides of the pool during a match. Matches can get rough, so players wear special caps with extra padding to protect their ears.

FOOTBALL

So as not to be seen as a rival to the FIFA World Cup, the men's football at the Olympics is open only to players aged 23 or under (except for three players who can be older). There is no age restriction for the women's teams. The USA has dominated the women's game, winning gold in four out of five Olympics.

In the 1972 gold medal basketball game, the USA was beating the Soviet Union by a single point with just one second remaining. But an official believed the time was wrong and had the clock reset so there were three seconds left, allowing the Soviets to score a last-second basket. The US players were so angry they refused to accept their silver medals, which are still lying in a bank vault in Switzerland.

With rules much like soccer, but with players using their hands rather than their feet to pass and score goals, handball was first played at the Olympics in 1936. It didn't prove a success, however, and was dropped from the Games until 1972.

THE DREAM TEAM

Perhaps the most famous team to take part in the Olympics was the US basketball team of 1992. This was the first Games since the rules had been changed allowing professional athletes to take part in the Olympics. Featuring all the US's top stars, including Michael Jordan and Magic Johnson, the US 'Dream Team' destroyed the opposition on its way to the gold medal.

MULTIDISCIPLINARY
EVENTS

For some athletes, competing in a single discipline just isn't enough of a challenge. Triathletes tackle three, pentathletes take on five, heptathletes go two better with seven, while decathletes compete in no less than ten.

THE BATTLING BROTHERS
As brothers, Britain's top two triathletes, Alastair (right) and Jonathan Brownlee (left) have a particularly personal rivalry. Alastair came out on top in 2012 winning the gold medal, while his brother claimed bronze.

The decathlon was introduced to the Olympic programme in 1904. This supremely arduous test of all-round sporting ability sees athletes perform in the 100m, long jump, shot put, high jump, 400m, 110m hurdles, discus, pole vault, javelin, and 1500m. A seven-event heptathlon for women was brought in for the 1984 games. Both events are staged over two days.

FIVE INTO ONE

In order to make the Modern Pentathlon more appealing to spectators, the competition was condensed down from five days to one day in 1996. The final events, running and shooting, have also been combined so that competitors now run four 800m laps, stopping in between to shoot at five targets using a laser gun.

The 1912 games saw the first staging of the five events of the Modern Pentathlon: fencing, 200m freestyle swimming, show jumping, running and shooting. It was called 'modern' to distinguish it from the Ancient Pentathlon which consisted of the long jump, javelin, discus, a short foot race and wrestling. A women's Modern Pentathlon was introduced for the 2000 games, along with the men and women's Triathlon.

To claim the 2012 heptathlon gold in London, Britain's Jessica Ennis (left) had to compete in the 100m hurdles, high jump, shot put, 200m, long jump, javelin and 800m. Points are awarded for each event and then added together. The highest overall score wins.

NON-STOP ACTION

Because the three events of the Olympic Triathlon – a 1500m swim, a 40km bike ride and a 10km run – take place one after the other, athletes can gain or lose time 'transitioning' between them: getting out of the water after the swim, putting on their helmets for the cycle ride (their shoes are attached to the pedals, as shown above) and then taking them off again and getting into their running shoes for the final stage.

THE CHANGING GAMES

Over the years, several new sports have been added to the Olympic programme, while others have been dropped. Sometimes the organisers have changed their minds and reinstated dropped sports at a later date.

UNUSUAL SPORTS

These are some of the more unusual sports that no longer feature at the Olympics:

- **Swimming obstacle race:** Competitors had to tackle a 200m course, swimming under and over boats and other obstacles. It was staged just once at the 1900 Olympics.
- **Tug of war:** This test of team strength was contested at the early games from 1900 to 1920.
- **Rope climb:** A rope-climbing competition was held between 1896 and 1932 as part of the gymnastic programme.
- **Duelling pistols:** At the 1912 games, competitors 'duelled' by firing a gun at a mannequin dressed in clothes from distances of 20–30m.
- **Live Pigeon Shooting:** Modern Olympic marksmen try to hit clay pigeons, but at the 1900 games they shot at the real thing. The winner managed to kill 21 birds.

At the very first ancient Olympics held in Greece in 776 BCE, there was just one event: a short foot race. Over the next few centuries various other races and events, including discus, long jump, boxing and chariot racing, were added. When the competition was revived in 1896, 241 male athletes competed in 43 events in nine sports: athletics, cycling, fencing, gymnastics, shooting, swimming, tennis, weightlifting and wrestling.

NEW SPORTS - GOLF

The Olympic golf tournament at Rio 2016 marks the first time the sport has been held at the games since 1904. Both men and women take part in four-day 'stroke-play' competitions. This means that the player who takes the fewest strokes to complete the holes wins the gold medal.

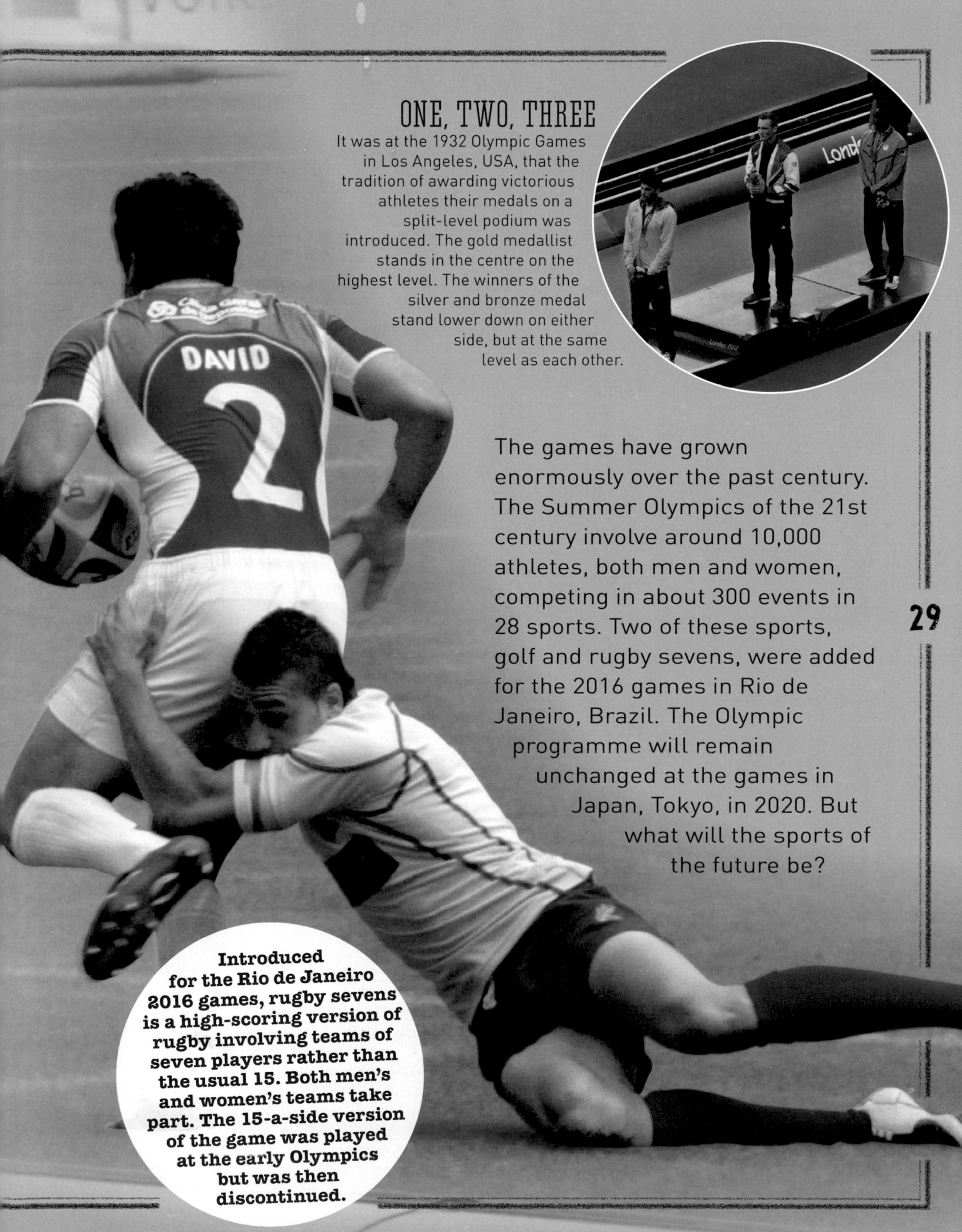

ONE, TWO, THREE

It was at the 1932 Olympic Games in Los Angeles, USA, that the tradition of awarding victorious athletes their medals on a split-level podium was introduced. The gold medallist stands in the centre on the highest level. The winners of the silver and bronze medal stand lower down on either side, but at the same level as each other.

The games have grown enormously over the past century. The Summer Olympics of the 21st century involve around 10,000 athletes, both men and women, competing in about 300 events in 28 sports. Two of these sports, golf and rugby sevens, were added for the 2016 games in Rio de Janeiro, Brazil. The Olympic programme will remain unchanged at the games in Japan, Tokyo, in 2020. But what will the sports of the future be?

Introduced for the Rio de Janeiro 2016 games, rugby sevens is a high-scoring version of rugby involving teams of seven players rather than the usual 15. Both men's and women's teams take part. The 15-a-side version of the game was played at the early Olympics but was then discontinued.

GLOSSARY

AERODYNAMIC
Specially shaped to move through the air quickly.

AQUATICS CENTRE
The venue for the Olympic swimming and diving competitions.

CEREMONY
A formal event, often involving several carefully planned procedures, staged to celebrate a particular occasion.

COX
In rowing races, the cox is a non-rowing crew member who sits at the back of the boat to steer it and encourage the rowers.

COXLESS
Rowing races that don't feature a cox, or steerer, in the boats.

DINGHY
A small boat with a mast and sails.

DRESSAGE
A form of horse riding in which the horse performs very precise, dance-like movements.

FIELD EVENTS
Throwing and jumping events that take place in the 'field' at the centre of the track in the Olympic Stadium.

FREESTYLE
A category of swimming races in which competitors may use any stroke they wish (in practice, they all use the fastest stroke, front crawl).

HOST CITY
Where an Olympic Games is staged.

MARKSMANSHIP
Skill and accuracy when using a firearm.

MULTIDISCIPLINARY
A sport involving several different events performed one after the other.

OLYMPIC PARK
The purpose-built area where most of the Olympic venues, as well as the athletes' housing, is located.

OLYMPIC STADIUM
The main sporting venue for the Olympic athletics (also known as track and field) events.

OPEN WATER
An outdoor body of water, such as a lake, sea or reservoir. Open water can be natural or man-made.

PODIUM
A platform on which athletes stand to receive their medals.

POMMEL HORSE

A piece of equipment on which male gymnasts perform routines.

SKULL

An oar used by rowers – it's also the name of a type of rowing boat. A single skull has one rower, a double skull has two rowers, and so on.

SYNCHRONIZED

A word that describes two or more actions performed in exactly the same way and at exactly the same time.

TRACK EVENTS

Running events that take place on the oval track at the Olympic Stadium.

VAULT

To jump over something. Gymnastics competitors jump over a piece of equipment called a vaulting horse.

VELODROME

An indoor venue where cycling events are staged on a sloping, wooden track.

WEBSITES

www.olympic.org
The official IOC website is packed full of features, statistics and news.

www.rio2016.com/en/the-games/olympic
Website dedicated to the 31st Summer Olympic Games in Rio de Janeiro, Brazil.

www.facebook.com/olympics
Videos, links and constant updates from the IOC's Facebook page.

www.activityvillage.co.uk/olympic-games
Olympic-themed games, puzzles, crafts, activities and worksheets from this great child-orientated website.

INDEX

32

ACKNOWLEDGEMENTS

First published in Great Britain in 2015 by Wayland

Copyright © Wayland, 2015

All rights reserved

Series editor: Elizabeth Brent

Produced by Tall Tree Ltd
Editor: Jon Richards
Designer: Gary Hyde, Ed Simkins, Jonathan Vipond

Dewey number: 796.4'8'098153-dc23

ISBN: 978 0 7502 9546 8

FSC®

Wayland, an imprint of Hachette Children's Group

Part of Hodder and Stoughton
Carmelite House, 50 Victoria Embankment, London EC4Y 0DZ

An Hachette UK Company
www.hachette.co.uk
www.hachettechildrens.co.uk

Printed and bound in China

10 9 8 7 6 5 4 3 2 1

Picture acknowledgements:
Every attempt has been made to clear copyright. Should there be any inadvertent omission, please apply to the publisher for rectification.

The website addresses (URLs) included in this book were valid at the time of going to press. However, it is possible that contents or addresses may have changed since the publication of this book. No responsibility for any such changes can be accepted by either the author or the Publisher.

The publisher would like to thank the following for their kind permission to reproduce their photographs:

Key: t-top, b-bottom, c-centre, l-left, r-right

All images are iStock.com unless otherwise stated.

Front Cover tl cdephotos, tr Shutterstock.com, b Getty Images/Bob Thomas. Back Cover l Madchester. Spine b johnthescone
Endpapers Dreamstime.com
p2 tl J. Brichto, pp2–3 c Madchester, 3 br Marie-Lan Nguyen
p4 bl Gerard McGovern, pp4–5 c J. Brichto, p5 bl Nick Webb, pp6–7 c Paul Rowlett, p7 tr Augustas Didžgalvis, p7 br Aurelien Guichard, p8 bl Dutch National Archives, p9 tr iamadonut, p9 br César, p10 b Bryan Allison, p11 cl

Craig Maccubbin, p12 b Marie-Lan Nguyen, p13 cl cdephotos, p14 bl Hpeterswald, pp14–15 c David Merrett, p15 br Getty Images/Ullstein Bild, p16 bl johnthescone, pp16–17 c p17 tr David Iliff, p18 bl Nizam Uddin, pp18–19 c Marie-Lan Nguyen, p19 tl Ken Hackman, US Air Force, p19 bl Martin Hesketh, pp20–21 c Madchester, p21 cl The US Army, p22 cl Henry Bucklow/Lazy Photography, pp22–23 c Craig Maccubbin, p23 tr Korean Culture and Information Service (Jang Miran), p23 br Ian Patterson, p24 cr akiwitz, pp24–25 c Ken Hackman, US Air Force, p25 tr Joel Solomon, p26 cl MartinPutz, pp26–27 c Adam Kerfoot-Roberts, pp28–29 c Discostu, p29 tr Darren Wilkinson, p31 tr Augustas Didžgalvis,